LE CORDON BLEU

HOME COLLECTION

CASSEROLES & ONE-POTS

MEREHURST

contents

recipe ratings ❄ *easy* ❄❄ *a little more care needed* ❄❄❄ *more care needed*

Braised beef in dill sauce

Slowly braised beef served with a creamy dill sauce makes a welcome change from the more traditional recipes for beef. Delicious served with crisp green vegetables and new potatoes.

Preparation time **25 minutes**
Total cooking time **2 hours 15 minutes**
Serves 4

1 kg (2 lb) tied joint of topside, top rump or silverside of beef
1 large carrot, quartered and cut into 4 cm (1¹/₂ inch) lengths
3 onions, quartered
1 stick celery, cut into 4 cm (1¹/₂ inch) lengths
1 large clove garlic, quartered
600 ml (20 fl oz) brown stock (see page 62)
1 small bay leaf
35 g (1¹/₄ oz) unsalted butter
30 g (1 oz) plain flour
150 g (5 oz) sour cream (see Chef's tips)
10 g (¹/₄ oz) chopped fresh dill or 3 g (¹/₈ oz) dried dill

1 Preheat the oven to moderate 180°C (350°F/Gas 4). On top of a stove, heat a little oil in a 2.5 litre capacity flameproof casserole dish until lightly hazing.

2 Place the beef in the casserole dish and brown quickly on all sides, including the ends, then transfer to a plate. Reduce the heat, add the carrot, onion and celery and cook until golden brown, turning frequently. Add the garlic, place the meat on the vegetables and pour in the stock—it will come about halfway up the meat. Season with salt and freshly ground black pepper and add the bay leaf. Bring to the boil, reduce the heat and cover with greaseproof paper and the lid. Simmer on top of the stove or bake in the oven for 1¹/₂ hours, turning the meat every 30 minutes. After 1¹/₂ hours,

check for tenderness by piercing with a sharp knife—cook for a further 15–30 minutes if necessary.

3 To make the sauce, melt the butter in a pan, add the flour and cook over low heat until the mixture turns from butter yellow to a pale straw colour. Remove from the heat and allow the mixture to cool.

4 Lift the meat out of the casserole dish onto a plate and cover with the greaseproof paper to keep moist. Strain 600 ml (20 fl oz) of the cooking liquid into a jug, discard the vegetables and bay leaf and skim the fat from the surface.

5 Gradually add most of the measured liquid to the butter and flour mixture and whisk until blended and smooth. Return to the stove, heat gently until lightly thickened, then increase the heat and bring to the boil, stirring. Cook, bubbling, for about 3 minutes, or until the sauce is reduced and lightly syrupy. Stir in the sour cream and reduce for a further 3 minutes, or until it lightly coats the back of a spoon. Stir in the dill, add more seasoning as necessary and cover.

6 Remove the string and slice the beef into 3 mm (¹/₄ inch) thick slices, then drizzle over the remaining cooking liquid to keep it moist. Pour a light coating of the sauce into a clean casserole or shallow serving dish. Place the meat in the dish and coat with the sauce. Cover and keep warm for 5 minutes before serving.

Chef's tips For a lighter sauce, use crème fraîche instead of sour cream.

To prepare this dish in advance, leave the sliced meat in a little cooking liquid and press a piece of buttered greaseproof paper onto the surface. To serve, warm the meat in its liquid and reheat the sauce.

Baked mushroom risotto

Traditional risotto is cooked on top of the stove and needs to be stirred constantly. This baked risotto, however, needs little attention and yet retains the beautiful taste and texture of the classically made version.

Preparation time **15 minutes + 2 hours soaking**
Total cooking time **1 hour**
Serves 6

15 g (¹/2 oz) dried morel or porcini mushrooms
875 ml (28 fl oz) chicken stock (see page 63) or
vegetable stock
60 g (2 oz) unsalted butter
I onion, finely chopped
I clove garlic, finely chopped
200 g (6¹/2 oz) flat mushrooms, thickly sliced
220 g (7 oz) Arborio rice
75 ml (2¹/2 fl oz) dry sherry
I sprig of fresh rosemary
2–3 tablespoons finely grated Parmesan
2 tablespoons coarsely grated Parmesan

1 Place the dried mushrooms in a deep bowl and pour over the boiling stock. Leave to soak for 2 hours, then strain through a fine sieve, reserving the liquid. Finely chop the mushrooms. Preheat the oven to slow 150°C (300°F/Gas 2). Place a 6 cm (2¹/2 inch) deep, 1.75 litre capacity, ovenproof dish in the oven to warm.

2 Melt the butter in a saucepan, add the onion and garlic and cook gently for 7 minutes. Stir in the fresh mushrooms and chopped dried mushrooms. Continue to cook gently for 15 minutes. Add the rice and stir for 1 minute. Pour in the reserved mushroom liquid, leaving the last tablespoon in the bowl with any sediment. Add the sherry and season with salt and pepper. Stir in the sprig of rosemary. Increase the heat, and when bubbles begin to show, transfer the mixture to the ovenproof dish. Cook on the middle shelf of the oven for about 15 minutes. Stir in the finely grated Parmesan and return to the oven for a further 20 minutes.

3 Stir the risotto as soon as it comes out of the oven. Discard the rosemary and season with salt and freshly ground black pepper to taste. Serve immediately, sprinkled with the remaining Parmesan.

Fish Dugléré

This dish takes its name from Adolphe Dugléré, a famous nineteenth-century French chef. The creamy white wine and tomato sauce may be served with any flatfish fillets.

*Preparation time **45 minutes***
*Total cooking time **55 minutes***
Serves 4

40 g (1¼ oz) unsalted butter
1 small onion, finely chopped
2 tablespoons finely chopped French shallots
4 flatfish fillets, such as brill, turbot, flounder or sole,
 about 185–250 g (6–8 oz) each
185 ml (6 fl oz) dry white wine
1 kg (2 lb) tomatoes, peeled, seeded and chopped
60 ml (2 fl oz) thick (double) cream
60 g (2 oz) unsalted butter, chilled and cut into cubes
1 tablespoon chopped fresh parsley

1 Rub a large frying pan with the butter. Sprinkle the bottom with the onion and shallots and lightly season with salt and pepper. Arrange the fish fillets on top and add the wine. Cover with a round of buttered baking paper. Place over medium heat and bring to a simmer. Cook for about 5–10 minutes, or until the fish has whitened and flakes when light pressure is applied. Remove the baking paper and transfer the fish to a small platter. Cover and keep warm.

2 Add the chopped tomatoes to the pan and increase the heat. Bring to the boil and cook until almost all the liquid has evaporated. Add the cream and return to the boil. Whisking constantly, gradually mix in the cubed butter. When the butter has all been incorporated, remove the pan from the heat and stir in the chopped parsley. Do not allow the sauce to boil again.

3 Drain any juices from the cooked fish into the tomato sauce. Season the sauce to taste with salt and freshly ground black pepper, then pour over the fish and serve immediately.

Chicken casserole with mushrooms and onions

The lovely flavours of the onions, bacon and mushrooms combine perfectly with the chicken to produce this popular casserole. This casserole will cook slowly in the oven, leaving you time to spend on other things.

Preparation time **25 minutes**
Total cooking time **1 hour 20 minutes**
Serves 4–6

12 pearl or pickling onions
60 g (2 oz) streaky bacon, rind removed and cut into 1 cm ($^{1}/_{2}$ inch) strips
80 g (2$^{3}/_{4}$ oz) unsalted butter (preferably clarified)
1.5 kg (3 lb) chicken, cut into 8 pieces (see page 62)
100 g (3$^{1}/_{4}$ oz) button mushrooms, quartered or whole if very small
30 g (1 oz) plain flour
600 ml (20 fl oz) chicken stock (see page 63)
bouquet garni (see page 63)
chopped fresh parsley, to garnish

1 Preheat the oven to warm 170°C (325°F/Gas 3). Place the onions in a small pan with the bacon strips, cover with cold water and bring to the boil. Drain and rinse with cold water. Melt 60 g (2 oz) of the butter in a 2.5 litre capacity, deep flameproof casserole dish on the stove. Add the chicken pieces, in batches, skin-side-down, and fry for 10 minutes, or until well browned. Remove from the pan and pat dry with paper towels.

2 Tip off the excess fat from the casserole dish, leaving about 2 tablespoons, then add the bacon, onions and mushrooms. Fry for 3 minutes, or until lightly browned, then remove. Melt the remaining butter in the casserole dish, add the flour and stir with a wooden spoon, scraping the base of the pan. Cook for 3 minutes, or until lightly golden. Gradually add the chicken stock and mix continuously until smooth and heated through. Do not boil.

3 Return the chicken to the pan with the bouquet garni, season with salt and pepper and place the bacon, onions and mushrooms on top. Bring just to the boil, cover and bake for 45 minutes, or until the chicken is tender and when pierced the juices are clear, not pink.

4 Transfer the chicken to a serving dish, then with a slotted spoon, lift out the bacon and vegetables and sprinkle over the chicken. Cover to keep warm and, if necessary, reduce the sauce to a syrupy consistency. Season the sauce to taste and pour over the chicken. Sprinkle with the parsley and serve with rice, pasta, dumplings or boiled potatoes.

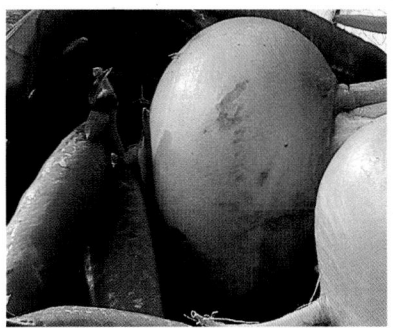

Navarin of lamb

This traditional French lamb and potato stew has existed for over one hundred and eighty years and is said to have been named after one of the main ingredients, 'navet', the French word for turnip. Other vegetables may also be added to the stew if desired, as in this recipe.

*Preparation time **45 minutes***
*Total cooking time **2 hours***
Serves 4

1 kg (2 lb) lamb shoulder, boned
80 ml (2³/4 fl oz) oil
40 g (1 1/4 oz) unsalted butter
1 large onion, finely chopped
1 tablespoon tomato paste
2 large tomatoes, peeled, seeded and chopped
3 cloves garlic, chopped
1 tablespoon plain flour
bouquet garni (see page 63)
150 g (5 oz) shelled peas
1 large carrot, cut into 5 cm (2 inch) pieces
2 turnips, peeled and quartered
12 new potatoes
1 tablespoon chopped fresh parsley

1 Preheat the oven to moderately hot 200°C (400°F/Gas 6). Trim off any excess fat from the meat and cut into 2.5 cm (1 inch) cubes. Heat the oil in a frying pan and cook the lamb in batches until brown.

Remove from the pan, drain off the oil, and set aside.

2 Place a 3 litre capacity flameproof casserole dish on top of the stove and melt the butter. Gently cook the onion for 5 minutes, without colouring. Add the tomato paste and cook over medium heat for 2 minutes. Add the tomatoes and cook for a further 3 minutes. Add the garlic and mix well. Add the lamb and any juices to the mixture and sprinkle the top with flour. Without mixing in the flour, place the dish in the oven for 5 minutes.

3 Remove the casserole from the oven and place over medium heat. Mix in the flour, then gradually add 1.5 litres boiling water. Mix well by scraping down the sides and bottom of the dish. Simmer for a few minutes, skimming off the foam, then add the bouquet garni, season to taste with salt and pepper, cover and return to the oven. Cook for 1 hour. Bring a large pan of salted water to the boil and cook the peas for 3 minutes. Drain, refresh with cold water, drain again, then set aside.

4 Remove the casserole from the oven and place over medium heat. Add the carrot, turnip and potatoes and cook for 15 minutes, then add the peas. Cook for a further 10–15 minutes, or until the meat and potatoes are tender. Remove the bouquet garni and discard, then season to taste. Stir in the parsley just before serving.

Beef with shallots, crème fraîche and anchovies

These succulent steaks, topped with a creamy anchovy sauce that is laced with brandy, make an ideal quick, yet quite special, supper dish.

*Preparation time **10 minutes + 15 minutes soaking***
*Total cooking time **10 minutes***
Serves 4

6 anchovy fillets
125 ml (4 fl oz) milk
1 tablespoon oil
4 sirloin steaks, about 175 g (5³/4 oz) each
30 g (1 oz) unsalted butter
3 French shallots, finely chopped
1 tablespoon brandy
125 ml (4 fl oz) crème fraîche
60 ml (2 fl oz) brown stock (see page 63)

1 Place the anchovy fillets in a small bowl and cover with the milk. Leave for 15 minutes, then drain. Discard the milk and finely chop the anchovies. Heat the oil in a large, heavy-based frying pan until it is just hazing. Add the steaks and fry for about 2 minutes on each side for medium. You may have to fry the steaks in two batches, depending on the size of the pan. Remove from the pan and keep warm.

2 Place the butter in the pan and stir until melted. Add the chopped shallots and cook, stirring, for 2–3 minutes, or until translucent. Stir in the brandy and boil for 30 seconds, then remove the pan from the heat. Add the crème fraîche, chopped anchovies, stock and a few twists of black pepper. Stir well, then return the pan to the heat and boil the sauce for 2 minutes. Remove from the heat.

3 To serve, divide the steaks between four warm plates and pour the hot sauce over the top.

Chef's tips Fillet or thin cuts of rump steak may be used in this recipe in place of the sirloin steaks.

Spicy chickpea stew

A chickpea stew with chilli, capsicums and tomatoes makes a warming winter dish.
Perfect for vegetarians, these nutty-flavoured chickpeas are delicious and low in fat.

*Preparation time **20 minutes + overnight soaking***
*Total cooking time **1 hour 40 minutes***
Serves 4–6

275 g (9 oz) dried chickpeas
2 tablespoons olive oil
1 large onion, chopped
3 cloves garlic, crushed
1/2–1 teaspoon chopped red chilli
1 large yellow capsicum (pepper), chopped
1 large red capsicum (pepper), chopped
400 g (12³/4 oz) can crushed Italian tomatoes
250 ml (8 fl oz) vegetable stock
3 tablespoons chopped fresh flat-leaf parsley

1 Place the chickpeas in a bowl and cover with plenty of cold water. Leave overnight, then drain. Place the chickpeas in a large pan of boiling water and cook for about 1 hour, or until tender. Drain well.

2 Heat the oil in a large pan and cook the onion over a medium heat for about 5 minutes, or until soft and lightly golden. Add the garlic and cook for 1 more minute.

3 Stir in the chilli and capsicums and cook, stirring occasionally, for about 5 minutes, or until the capsicums are soft. Add the tomatoes, stock and chickpeas and bring to the boil.

4 Reduce the heat and simmer for 25 minutes, or until the chickpeas are tender and the sauce has reduced and thickened slightly. Just before serving, stir in the parsley.

Venison casserole

Venison is the most common large game and has a distinctive gamey flavour. In this recipe, the venison is slowly cooked to perfection with onions, mushrooms and garlic in red wine. It is then combined with redcurrant jelly and juniper berries to produce a truly memorable dish.

Preparation time **30 minutes**
Total cooking time **2 hours**
Serves 4

**750 g (1 1/2 lb) braising venison off the bone
    or 2 kg (4 lb) venison cutlets**
185 g (6 oz) pearl or pickling onions
2 tablespoons olive oil
250 g (8 oz) button mushrooms
1 clove garlic, crushed
1 tablespoon plain flour
250 ml (8 fl oz) red wine
1 tablespoon redcurrant jelly
6 juniper berries, crushed

1 Preheat the oven to warm 170°C (325°F/Gas 3). If using venison off the bone, cut the meat into 4 cm (1 1/2 inch) pieces.

2 Place the onions in a small pan with just enough cold water to cover them. Bring to the boil, reduce the heat, simmer for 2 minutes, then drain. Heat the oil in a 2.5 litre capacity flameproof casserole dish over high heat. When it is very hot, add the meat in batches and fry for 1–2 minutes each side, or until brown on all sides. Remove the meat from the dish and keep warm.

3 Add the onions to the casserole dish and toss gently in the oil until they just begin to colour. Add the mushrooms and garlic and cook for about 1 minute. Sprinkle in the flour and cook, stirring, for 1 minute. Stir in the wine, 250 ml (8 fl oz) water and some salt and bring to the boil. Return the meat to the dish, cover and place in the oven to cook for 1 1/2 hours.

4 Remove the casserole from the oven and strain off the liquid into a small pan. Bring to the boil and cook for 1 minute to reduce the liquid. Stir in the redcurrant jelly, add the juniper berries and return to the boil. Season to taste with salt and freshly ground black pepper, then pour the liquid over the casserole. Return to the oven and cook for a further 15 minutes to heat through. Serve the casserole piping hot with a potato and celeriac purée.

Cioppino

This superb Italian-sounding dish is said to have been created in San Francisco by Italian immigrants.
A combination of fish and seafood with tomatoes and herbs, it is delicious served with crusty bread.

Preparation time 45 minutes
Total cooking time 35 minutes
Serves 6–8

750 ml (24 fl oz) white wine
2 onions, finely chopped
2 bay leaves
4 sprigs of fresh thyme
1 kg (2 lb) mussels, scrubbed and beards removed
30 g (1 oz) fresh basil
80 ml (2³/4 fl oz) olive oil
1 green capsicum (pepper), chopped
1 stick celery, chopped
1 carrot, chopped
4 cloves garlic, chopped
2 tablespoons tomato paste
3 x 400 g (12fl fl oz) cans chopped Italian tomatoes
2 x 250 g (8 oz) frozen lobster tails, thawed
500 g (1 lb) white fish fillets
500 g (1 lb) frozen crab claws, thawed
1 kg (2 lb) large raw prawns, shells on
500 g (1 lb) scallops
4 cloves garlic, finely chopped
2 tablespoons extra virgin olive oil

1 Place the wine, half the onion, one bay leaf, two sprigs of thyme and the mussels in a large pan. Cover, bring to the boil and cook for 5 minutes. Remove the mussels from the pan with a slotted spoon and discard any that have not opened. Strain and reserve the cooking liquid.

2 Separate the leaves from the stems of basil and set aside. Make a herb bundle by tying the basil stems, remaining thyme and bay leaf together with string.

3 Heat the oil in a large pan and cook the remaining onion, capsicum, celery, carrot and garlic for 3 minutes. Add the tomato paste and cook for a further 2 minutes, stirring regularly. Add the tomatoes, herb bundle and mussel liquid to the pan and bring to the boil. Reduce the heat and simmer for 10 minutes.

4 Meanwhile, with a large sharp knife, cut each lobster tail into three or four pieces. Cut the fish into bite-sized pieces and crack the crab claws with a nutcracker or mallet. Remove the mussels from their shells. Peel and devein the prawns, keeping the tails intact.

5 Remove the herb bundle, then add all the seafood except the mussels to the pan. Simmer for 10 minutes, add the mussels and heat through.

6 To make the basil sauce, finely chop the reserved basil leaves and combine with the garlic and olive oil. Season the Cioppino to taste, then stir in the basil sauce and serve with thick slices of crusty bread.

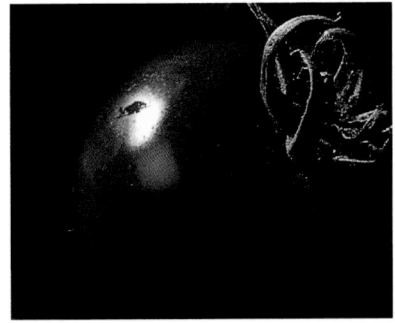

Sautéed rabbit with mushrooms

Rabbit meat is very lean, which makes this tasty dish even more attractive. Combined with mushrooms, shallots and tomatoes, slowly cooked in white wine and enhanced with the flavour of fresh herbs, this rabbit casserole is perfect for a special occasion.

Preparation time 25 minutes
Total cooking time 1 hour 20 minutes
Serves 4

1.8 kg (3 lb 10 oz) rabbit, cut into 8 pieces
80 g (2³/4 oz) unsalted butter
130 g (4¹/4 oz) mushrooms, sliced
2 French shallots, chopped
250 ml (8 fl oz) white wine
3 large tomatoes, peeled, seeded and chopped
500 ml (16 fl oz) brown stock (see page 63)
bouquet garni (see page 63)
1–2 teaspoons chopped fresh tarragon
1 tablespoon chopped fresh chervil

1 Season the rabbit with salt and pepper and preheat the oven to moderate 180°C (350°F/Gas 4). Melt half the butter in a large flameproof casserole dish over medium heat and brown the rabbit in batches. Remove the meat from the dish and set aside. Discard the butter left in the dish, then return the dish to the heat and add the remaining butter. Add the mushrooms and cook for 3 minutes, then add the shallot and cook for 3 minutes. Add the wine and continue cooking for 3 minutes, or until almost all the liquid has evaporated.

2 Add the tomato and mix well. Bring to the boil, reduce the heat and simmer for 10 minutes. Add the stock and bouquet garni and return to the boil. Allow to boil for 5 minutes, skimming off any foam or fat that comes to the surface.

3 Return the rabbit to the dish and bring to a simmer. Cover and bake for 20–25 minutes, or until the rabbit is tender. To test the meat, pierce a thick piece with a fork and lift it up. If tender, it should slide easily from the bone. Transfer the rabbit to a serving platter, cover and keep warm. Place the casserole dish on the stove top and remove the bouquet garni. Bring the sauce to the boil and cook for 5–10 minutes, skimming as necessary. Adjust the seasoning and check the consistency of the sauce. If the sauce is not thick enough, continue to boil for about 5 minutes, or until it is the desired consistency.

4 Stir in the chopped tarragon and chervil and pour the sauce over the rabbit. Serve immediately.

Beef à la flamande

This traditional Flemish recipe consists of tender beef and onions that have been slowly stewed in beer with a little sugar. It makes a satisfying warming dish for a cold winter's evening.

Preparation time **30 minutes**
Total cooking time **3 hours**
Serves 4

1 kg (2 lb) piece chuck steak or topside beef, cut into
**   eight 1 cm (¹/2 inch) thick slices**
3 tablespoons lard or oil
4 small onions, thinly sliced
3 tablespoons plain flour
1 tablespoon tomato paste
1 litre beer (not bitter)
bouquet garni (see page 63)
3 juniper berries
1 tablespoon sugar
1.25 litres brown stock (see page 63)

1 Preheat the oven to moderate 180°C (350°F/Gas 4). Season the beef slices with salt and pepper. Melt the lard or oil in a large flameproof casserole dish and fry the meat, in batches, over high heat until browned, remove from the pan and set aside. Reduce the heat and add the onion to the dish. Cook gently for about 10–15 minutes, or until soft and golden brown.

2 Add the flour and tomato paste and cook, stirring, for about 3 minutes over low heat. Gradually add the beer, then the bouquet garni, juniper berries and sugar, increase the heat and bring to the boil, stirring. Add the stock and return to the boil, then add the beef and simmer for 5 minutes. Skim off any foam that floats to the top. Cover and bake for 1¹/2–2 hours.

3 To test if the beef is tender, remove a piece and cut it. If it is still a little tough, return it to the oven and bake for another 15 minutes. Once the beef is tender, remove it from the dish, cover and set aside. Bring the sauce to the boil on top of the stove and skim off any foam. Cook for about 10 minutes or until it is thick enough to coat the back of a spoon. Season to taste. Arrange the beef on a platter and cover with the sauce just before serving.

Veal kidneys sautéed in white wine

A simple and delicious dish of veal kidneys cooked with wine, shallots and herbs. The recipe may be adjusted according to personal preference by adding mustard or cream. Use these variations to transform this one recipe into three different meals.

*Preparation time **25 minutes***
*Total cooking time **25 minutes***
Serves 4

3 veal kidneys, outer fat removed
60 g (2 oz) unsalted butter
4 French shallots, finely chopped
250 ml (8 fl oz) white wine
500 ml (16 fl oz) brown stock (see page 63)
1 tablespoon chopped fresh parsley

1 Cut the kidneys in half and remove the central core, then cut them into bite-sized pieces. Melt two thirds of the butter in a flameproof casserole dish over high heat and brown the kidneys in batches for 2–3 minutes— taking care not to overcook. Remove the kidneys from

the dish, set aside and keep warm.

2 Reduce the heat to medium and, using the same dish, melt the remaining butter. Add the shallots and cook for 1 minute, without colouring, then add the wine and cook for about 5 minutes, or until it is almost completely evaporated. Add the stock and cook for a further 8–10 minutes, or until the sauce is thick enough to coat the back of a spoon. Season to taste with salt and pepper. Add the kidneys and heat through for 1 minute without boiling. Remove from the heat, stir in the parsley and serve.

Chef's tip This is a basic recipe that can be changed to suit different tastes. A tablespoon of mustard can be added to the sauce before being seasoned. For a richer dish, the stock can be replaced by cream, with or without the addition of the mustard.

White bean stew with fennel sausages

Dried cannellini beans—full of protein, calcium and iron—are cooked with aniseed-flavoured Italian sausages in a creamy herb sauce, making this stew a complete meal.

Preparation time **25 minutes**
Total cooking time **1 hour 30 minutes**
Serves 4

375 g (12 oz) dried cannellini beans
I small onion, diced
I small carrot, diced
I small celery stick, diced
sprig of fresh thyme
sprig of fresh rosemary
I teaspoon black peppercorns
4 Italian-style sausages with fennel
60 ml (2 fl oz) thick (double) cream
chopped fresh parsley, to garnish

HERB BUTTER
I clove garlic, roughly chopped
I tablespoon chopped fresh parsley
I tablespoon fresh rosemary leaves
I tablespoon fresh thyme leaves
120 g (4 oz) unsalted butter, softened

1 Place the beans and vegetables in a large flameproof casserole dish with the sprigs of thyme and rosemary. Wrap the peppercorns in a piece of muslin and add to the dish. Cover with 1.5 litres cold water. Place on the stove and bring to the boil, then reduce the heat to low and simmer for 55 minutes.

2 To make the herb butter, use a mortar and pestle or a blender to purée the garlic, parsley, rosemary, thyme and butter until smooth. Season to taste with salt and pepper and set aside.

3 Preheat the oven to moderate 180°C (350°F/Gas 4). Heat a little oil in a frying pan and brown the sausages. Cut diagonally into four pieces and add to the beans after they have finished simmering. Cover and bake in the oven for 30 minutes, or until the beans are tender. There should be just enough liquid left to cover the beans. If not, add more water.

4 Remove the sausages and set aside. Remove the sachet of peppercorns and the sprigs of herbs and discard. Mix in the herb butter and the cream and season to taste. Arrange the sausages on top, sprinkle with some chopped parsley and serve.

Beef casserole with herb scones

Just below the well-risen, golden brown scones is a rich, tender beef and mushroom casserole, which is guaranteed to liven up a cold winter's day.

*Preparation time **30 minutes***
*Total cooking time **2 hours***
Serves 4–6

2 tablespoons olive oil
750 g (1 1/2 lb) chuck steak or good-quality braising or
   stewing steak, cut into 2.5 cm (1 inch) cubes
2 onions, thinly sliced
1 clove garlic, crushed
1 tablespoon plain flour
200 ml (6 1/2 fl oz) red wine
1 teaspoon tomato paste
250 g (8 oz) flat mushrooms, quartered

HERB SCONES
250 g (8 oz) self-raising flour
1/4 teaspoon salt
60 g (2 oz) unsalted butter, chilled and cut into cubes
1 tablespoon chopped fresh herbs, such as parsley,
   rosemary or thyme
115 ml (3 3/4 fl oz) buttermilk (see Chef's tip)
1 egg, beaten

1 Preheat the oven to slow 150°C (300°F/Gas 2). Heat the oil in a flameproof casserole dish until it is very hot. Brown the meat in batches, taking care not to overcrowd the pan, for 3–4 minutes each side, then remove from the dish and set aside.

2 Add the onion to the dish with the garlic and cook for 2 minutes. Sprinkle the flour on top and stir in with a wooden spoon, scraping the base of the dish. Cook for about 1 minute, stirring continuously, until the mixture is golden brown. Gradually stir in the wine, 200 ml (6 1/2 fl oz) water and the tomato paste, and season with salt and freshly ground black pepper. Continue stirring until the mixture begins to thicken, then return the meat to the pan, add the mushrooms and stir to the boil. Cover and either cook gently on the stove or in the oven for 1 1/2 hours.

3 Begin preparing the herb scones no more than about 10 minutes before the beef has finished cooking. Sift the flour and salt into a wide bowl, then add the butter and rub in with a flicking action of the thumb across the tips of the fingers. When the mixture resembles fine breadcrumbs, add the herbs. Stir in the buttermilk, using a round-bladed knife, until the flour has disappeared and the mixture is in large lumps, then draw together quickly into a rough ball. Place on a lightly floured surface and knead quickly until just smooth. Roll or pat out the dough with the palm of your hand to a 1.5 cm (5/8 inch) thickness, then cut out about ten circles using a 5 cm (2 inch) cutter.

4 Remove the casserole from the oven, then increase the temperature to moderately hot 200°C (400°F/Gas 6). Arrange the scones on the surface of the casserole and brush the tops with the egg. Place the casserole at the top of the oven, uncovered, to cook for 12 minutes, or until the scones have risen and turned golden brown.

Chef's tip If you can't buy buttermilk, add 1 teaspoon of lemon juice to fresh milk.

Paella

A classic Spanish dish consisting of rice, saffron and olive oil, often combined with chicken, seafood, pork and chorizo, as well as garlic, onions, tomatoes and peas. The name is derived from the large two-handled dish that it is traditionally cooked and served in.

Preparation time **30 minutes**
Total cooking time **1 hour**
Serves 4–6

2 pinches of saffron threads
3 tablespoons olive oil
4 small skinless chicken thigh fillets, each cut
   into 2 long pieces
1 large onion, sliced
300 g (10 oz) long-grain rice
3 tomatoes, peeled, seeded and roughly chopped or
   250 g (8 oz) can chopped Italian tomatoes, drained
2 cloves garlic, crushed
550 ml (18 fl oz) chicken stock (see page 63) or
   vegetable stock
300 g (10 oz) mussels, scrubbed and beards removed
8 large raw prawns, shells on
150 g (5 oz) salmon, cod or haddock, cut into
   3 cm (1 1/4 inch) pieces
90 g (3 oz) frozen peas
80 g (2 3/4 oz) chorizo, ham or smoked bacon, cut into
   5 mm (1/4 inch) slices
1 red capsicum (pepper), cut into 2.5 cm (1 inch)
   lengths and thinly sliced
chopped fresh parsley, to garnish

1 Soak the saffron threads in 2 tablespoons hot water. Heat the oil in a wide, deep ovenproof frying pan or paella pan, 30–35 cm (12–14 inches) in diameter. When it is lightly hazing, add the chicken. Cook over medium heat for about 10 minutes, turning until golden brown on all sides. Remove from the pan and set aside.

2 Reduce the heat, add the onion and cook for about 3–4 minutes, or until soft. Add the rice and cook, stirring, for 2 minutes. Add the tomatoes, garlic and stock and bring to the boil. Reduce the heat and stir in half of the chicken, mussels, prawns and fish with all of the peas, chorizo, red capsicum, saffron and its soaking liquid. Season well with salt and pepper.

3 Arrange the remaining seafood and meat on top and cover with greaseproof paper and a lid. Cook over low heat, or in a warm 160°C (315°F/Gas 2–3) oven, for 30 minutes, or until the rice is tender and the liquid has been absorbed. Discard any unopened mussels.

4 Don't stir the Paella while it cooks as this will break up the fish and make the finished dish look messy. You may also need to add a little extra water when the liquid has been absorbed if the rice is not cooked. Sprinkle with the chopped parsley and serve immediately.

Chef's tip If any of the mussels appears unusually heavy, throw it away as it is may be full of grit.

Lancashire hot pot

A traditional regional British casserole, its exceptional flavour comes from the meat cooked on the bone adding to the flavour of the stock as it cooks.

*Preparation time **30 minutes***
*Total cooking time **2 hours 20 minutes***
Serves 4

1 kg (2 lb) middle neck of lamb chops
20 g (3/4 oz) unsalted butter
900 g (1 lb 13 oz) potatoes, peeled
2 large onions, finely sliced
2 carrots, sliced into 2 mm (1/8 inch) thick rounds
1/2 teaspoon chopped fresh thyme
1 bay leaf
400 ml (12 3/4 fl oz) brown stock (see page 63)
60 g (2 oz) unsalted butter, melted

1 Preheat the oven to moderate 180°C (350°F/Gas 4). Brush a 3.5 litre capacity ovenproof casserole dish with butter. Trim off the excess fat from the lamb, melt the butter in a frying pan and, over high heat, quickly fry the chops until lightly browned and just sealed, but not cooked through. Remove from the pan and transfer the chops to a plate.

2 Slice the potatoes into 2 mm (1/8 inch) thick rounds and cover the base of the casserole dish with about a third of the slices. Season lightly with salt and pepper. Place the chops neatly on the potato, scatter with the onion, carrot and thyme, season lightly and add the bay leaf. Put the remaining potato slices into the dish, neatly overlapping the very top layer. Pour on enough of the stock to come up to just under the top layer by pouring the stock down one side of the dish so that the top layer is not wet. Brush well with melted butter and season lightly with salt and pepper. Cover and cook on the middle shelf of the oven for 1 1/2 hours.

3 Remove the lid, then add a little more stock or water if the liquid has been taken up by the potato and you would like it to be moister. Return the dish to the oven for about 45 minutes, uncovered, or until the meat is cooked and the potato top is crisp and brown. Serve hot with green vegetables of your choice.

Chef's tips Do not slice the peeled potato until required or it will discolour. Also, do not keep sliced potato in cold water, as the starch that is needed to help thicken the hot pot will be washed out.

If you wish, add one lamb's kidney, halved, trimmed of its core and cut into 1 cm (1/2 inch) pieces. Scatter it raw onto the lamb as it goes into the casserole dish.

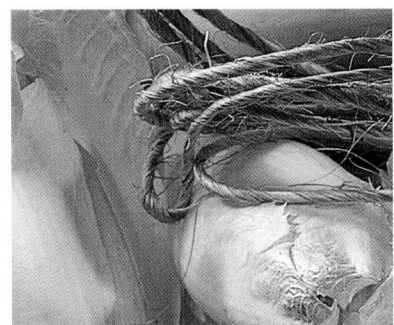

Braised witlof

*A vegetable that is wonderful braised, even though it is often thought
of as being a salad ingredient.*

*Preparation time **15 minutes***
*Total cooking time **1 hour 30 minutes***
Serves 4

60 g (2 oz) unsalted butter
4 witlof (chicory)
500 ml (16 fl oz) chicken stock (see page 63) or water
1 tablespoon lemon juice
1/2 teaspoon sugar
1 teaspoon chopped fresh parsley

1 Preheat the oven to moderate 180°C (350°F/Gas 4). Grease a flameproof baking dish with one third of the butter. Remove any blemished outer leaves from the witlof and trim and core the root end. This removes some of the bitterness. Wash and place in the dish.

2 Add the stock or water with the lemon juice to the dish. Season lightly with salt, pepper and the sugar and bring to the boil on the stove top. Remove and cover with buttered greaseproof paper and then foil. Transfer to the oven and bake for about 1–1 1/4 hours, or until the witlof are tender. Remove and place on a rack to drain, reserving the cooking liquid. Cook the liquid over high heat until syrupy. Set aside and keep warm.

3 Once the witlof have cooled, lightly tie in the middle with some kitchen string. Heat the remaining butter in a non-stick frying pan and brown the witlof on all sides.

4 Remove the string, place the witlof in a serving dish and cover with the reduced cooking liquid. Sprinkle with the parsley.

Chef's tip Before tying the witlof with the string, you could wrap a slice of bacon around the middle.

Fricassee of salmon and turbot

While chicken or veal fricassees are probably the most common, fish and seafood that have been sautéed and then cooked in white wine and cream may also be referred to as fricassees, as in this case.

*Preparation time **15 minutes***
*Total cooking time **50 minutes***
Serves 4

100 g (3¹/4 oz) unsalted butter
8 scallops, shelled and dark vein removed
8 large raw prawns, peeled and deveined
200 g (6¹/2 oz) salmon fillet, cut into 8 pieces
200 g (6¹/2 oz) sole or turbot fillet, cut into 8 pieces
2 French shallots, finely chopped
I carrot, cut into julienne strips (see Chef's tips)
I leek, white part only, cut into julienne strips
60 ml (2 fl oz) white wine
250 ml (8 fl oz) cream
2 tablespoons snipped fresh chives

1 Melt 20 g (3/4 oz) of the butter in a frying pan over high heat and lightly brown the scallops. Repeat with the prawns, salmon and sole or turbot, browning each separately in 20 g (3/4 oz) of butter. Drain on paper towels and set aside.

2 Melt the remaining butter in a large flameproof casserole dish over low heat. Add the shallots and cook for 2–3 minutes without colouring, then add the carrot and leek strips. Cover and cook over low heat for about 8 minutes. Add the wine and cook for 3 minutes, or until reduced in volume by three quarters—leaving you about 1 tablespoon of liquid. Stir in the cream and cook for a further 5 minutes. Gently mix in the seafood, season to taste with salt and freshly ground black pepper and simmer for 2–3 minutes. Remove from the heat and stir in the chives. Serve immediately.

Chef's tips The salmon can be replaced with any firm-fleshed fish.

For a Mediterranean flavour, add a pinch of saffron threads soaked in a tablespoon of hot water to the sauce.

Julienne strips are even-sized strips of vegetables, the size and shape of matchsticks.

Beef stroganoff

Thin strips of beef fillet, shallots and mushrooms sautéed in butter and served in a sour cream sauce.

Preparation time **20 minutes**
Total cooking time **30 minutes**
Serves 4

3 tablespoons olive oil
600 g (1 1/4 lb) beef fillet, cut into 5 x 1 cm
  (2 x 1/2 inch) strips
30 g (1 oz) unsalted butter
3 large shallots, finely chopped
1 tablespoon paprika
50 g (1 3/4 oz) mushrooms, thinly sliced
25 ml (3/4 fl oz) white wine vinegar
50 ml (1 3/4 fl oz) brandy
250 ml (8 fl oz) chicken stock (see page 63)
200 ml (6 1/2 fl oz) sour cream
20 g (3/4 oz) pickled gherkins, cut into julienne strips
  (see Chef's tip)
20 g (3/4 oz) cooked beetroot, cut into julienne strips

1 Heat the oil in a frying pan over high heat until very hot. Add the meat and fry in batches for 3–5 minutes, stirring continuously, until lightly browned. Remove from the pan, set aside and keep warm.
2 Melt the butter in the pan, add the shallots and cook for 2 minutes or until soft but not coloured. Stir in the paprika for 45 seconds, then add the mushrooms and cook over high heat until dry. Add the vinegar and cook for about 1 minute, or until the pan is nearly dry. Add the brandy, cook until the liquid is reduced to half, then add the stock and reduce to half again. Finally, add half the sour cream and return the meat to the pan to reheat. Serve with the Vegetable pilaf, dotted with the remaining sour cream and the gherkins and beetroot.

Chef's tip Julienne strips are even-sized vegetable strips, the size and shape of matchsticks.

Vegetable pilaf

This brightly coloured vegetable and rice dish makes a very good accompaniment to beef stroganoff.

Preparation time **10 minutes**
Total cooking time **30 minutes**
Serves 4–6

20 g (3/4 oz) unsalted butter
1 onion, finely chopped
200 g (6 1/2 oz) long-grain rice
375 ml (12 fl oz) chicken stock (see page 63)
1/2 carrot, peeled and finely diced
bouquet garni (see page 63)
1 zucchini (courgette), finely diced
50 g (1 3/4 oz) frozen baby peas, thawed

1 Melt the butter in a large heavy-based pan, add the onion and cook for 1 minute until softened. Add the rice and stir to coat in the butter. Pour in the stock and add the carrot and bouquet garni. Bring to the boil, reduce the heat to low, cover and simmer for about 25 minutes, or until the rice is tender and all the liquid has been absorbed. Remove the bouquet garni.
2 Fold the zucchini and peas into the rice. Cover and leave for 3–4 minutes before serving warm with the Beef stroganoff.

Beef stroganoff (bottom left) and Vegetable pilaf

Blanquette de veau

A blanquette is a classic French 'bourgeois' dish, which derives its name from 'blanc', the French word for white. It is always made from white meat cooked in a white stock or water, then enriched with cream.

*Preparation time **20 minutes***
*Total cooking time **2 hours 10 minutes***
Serves 4

1.4 kg (2 lb 12 oz) veal stewing meat, such as shoulder
I carrot, quartered
I small onion, quartered
I stick celery, quartered
bouquet garni (see page 63)
I teaspoon salt
10–12 peppercorns
150 g (5 oz) pearl or pickling onions
250 g (8 oz) button mushrooms, sliced
I teaspoon lemon juice
55 g (1¾ oz) unsalted butter
30 g (1 oz) plain flour
300 ml (10 fl oz) thick (double) cream

1 Remove excess fat from the veal and cut into 3 cm (1¼ inch) cubes. Place in a large flameproof casserole dish with the carrot, onion, celery, bouquet garni, salt and peppercorns. Cover with about 500 ml (16 fl oz) cold water and bring to the boil on the stove top, skimming off any foam that comes to the surface. Reduce the heat and simmer for 1½ hours, or until tender, skimming regularly. Add boiling water if necessary to keep the meat covered in liquid.

2 Cook the onions for 10 minutes in boiling salted water, drain well and set aside. Cook the mushrooms for about 5 minutes in 2–3 tablespoons boiling salted water with the lemon juice and just under half of the butter. Drain well and set aside.

3 After 1½ hours, check if the meat is cooked by piercing it with a fork—it should not resist and should slip easily from the fork. Remove the veal from the cooking liquid. Strain the liquid, discarding the solids, return to the heat and cook for 30 minutes, or until it has reduced by two thirds of its volume, skimming off excess fat. Cool slightly. Melt the remaining butter in a large pan, add the flour and cook for 1 minute. Stir in the reduced liquid and cook over low heat, whisking constantly, until the sauce has thickened. Add the cream, mix until smooth and season to taste.

4 Add the meat, onions and mushrooms to the pan and simmer for 5 minutes. Serve in a deep serving dish.

Cassoulet

Haricot beans are the essential ingredient in this dish from Languedoc and give the cassoulet its creaminess. Some sort of meat, depending on the region, and a gratin topping are added near the end of cooking. The word cassoulet comes from 'cassole', an earthenware pot traditionally used for cooking this dish.

Preparation time 1 hour 30 minutes + soaking overnight
Total cooking time 4 hours 30 minutes
Serves 4–6

250 g (8 oz) dried haricot beans (navy beans), soaked overnight in cold water
100 g (3¼ oz) fresh pork rind
100 g (3¼ oz) slab bacon
½ carrot
½ onion, stuck with a clove
2 bouquet garni (see page 63)
I clove garlic
40 g (1¼ oz) goose fat, duck fat or lard
200 g (6½ oz) boneless lamb shoulder, cut into 8 pieces
200 g (6½ oz) boneless pork shoulder, cut into 8 pieces
I small onion, chopped
2 tomatoes, peeled, seeded and cubed or I tablespoon tomato paste
I clove garlic, crushed
300 g (10 oz) fresh garlic sausage, sliced
4 small fresh Toulouse or pork sausages
2 legs duck or goose confit or I cooked duck Maryland (leg quarter), about 360 g (11½ oz) altogether, cut into 2 pieces
90 g (3 oz) fresh breadcrumbs

1 Preheat the oven to moderate 180°C (350°F/Gas 4). Rinse the soaked beans and cover generously with fresh cold water in a large pan. Add the pork rind and slab bacon and bring to the boil. As soon as it reaches the boil, remove from the heat, strain and refresh in cold water. Cover once more with fresh water, return to the heat and add the carrot, cloved onion, 1 bouquet garni and the garlic. Simmer for about 1½ hours (do not add salt, as this will interfere with the cooking of the beans and make them tough).

2 While the beans are simmering, melt 25 g (¾ oz) of the goose fat, duck fat or lard in a large flameproof casserole dish. Season the lamb shoulder and pork shoulder and brown in the casserole dish. Remove and set aside. In the same dish, cook the chopped onion until soft but not coloured. Add the tomato or tomato paste, crushed garlic and the second bouquet garni. Heat until bubbling, return the meat to the casserole dish, cover and place in the oven for 1 hour to 1½ hours, or until the meat is tender. Remove the meat from the casserole.

3 Reduce the oven temperature to warm 160°C (315°F/Gas 2–3). Add the garlic sausage, Toulouse sausages and confit to the casserole, bring to a simmer on the stove, then cook in the oven for 20 minutes. Transfer the confit and the sausages to a bowl and keep warm and set the sauce aside. Reduce the oven temperature to slow 150°C (300°F/Gas 2).

4 When the beans are almost cooked (they should be tender with a slight resistance), drain and add the beans' cooking liquid to the reserved sauce in the casserole dish. Remove and discard the vegetables and bouquet garni. Remove the slab bacon and pork rind and allow to cool. Keeping the bacon and pork separate, cut into bite-sized pieces.

5 Warm a large, ovenproof serving dish. Cover the bottom with some of the pork rind and then cover with a layer of beans. Add the lamb shoulder, pork shoulder, sausages, confit and about 250–375 ml (8–12 fl oz) of the reserved liquid. Cover with another layer of beans and top with the pieces of bacon, the remaining pork rind and liquid. Sprinkle with breadcrumbs and drizzle with the remaining melted goose fat. Bake for 1 hour, or until the breadcrumbs are lightly coloured, then serve.

Traditional corned beef with vegetables and dumplings

Delicious pink corned beef served with onions, carrots, turnips and light dumplings cooked in a well-flavoured beef stock. The marrow may be extracted from the bone with a teaspoon and is particularly good sprinkled with a little salt.

Preparation time **20 minutes + 3 hours soaking**
Total cooking time **4 hours 30 minutes**
Serves 6

1 kg (2 lb) piece of corned beef (salt beef)
6 x 5 cm (2 inch) pieces of marrowbone
bouquet garni (see page 63)
6 peppercorns
1/2 onion
6 onions, quartered
4 large carrots, quartered
2 turnips, quartered
2 teaspoons chopped fresh parsley

DUMPLINGS
225 g (7 1/4 oz) self-raising flour
pinch of salt
50 g (1 3/4 oz) suet, coarsely grated
115 ml (3 3/4 fl oz) cold water

1 Soak the beef in cold water for at least 3 hours, remove and rinse.
2 Place the marrowbones and beef in a large pan, cover with water and bring to the boil slowly, skimming off the foam as necessary.
3 Reduce the heat to a simmer. Add the bouquet garni, peppercorns and the 1/2 onion. Partially cover the pan and simmer for 3 hours. Check regularly and skim off any fat and scum. Remove and discard the bouquet garni, peppercorns and onion. Add the quartered onions, carrot and turnip and simmer for 40 minutes.
4 Begin to prepare the dumplings 30 minutes before the beef is cooked. Sift the flour and salt into a bowl and stir in the suet. Make a well in the centre, add a little water, and draw in the flour using a knife. Add enough of the water to make a soft, but not sticky dough, then knead gently until smooth. Shape, with floured hands, into about 20 dumplings. Add to the pan of beef and cook for about 20 minutes, or until they float and have puffed up. Remove with a slotted spoon.
5 Place the beef in a large dish surrounded with vegetables from the pot, dumplings and marrowbones. Cover and keep warm. Reduce the stock for about 30 minutes, skimming as necessary, until it has a good flavour. Ladle onto the meat and sprinkle with parsley.

Chef's tip These dumplings could be made to be served with other casseroles. Simply poach in 550 ml (18 fl oz) of simmering beef stock or well-salted water.

Steak au poivre

A simple method for a traditional French pepper steak with quite controversial origins. At least four chefs claimed to have invented this dish at various times between 1905 and 1930!

Preparation time **10 minutes**
Total cooking time **30 minutes**
Serves 4

4 x 150–180 g (5–5³⁄4 oz) fillet or rump steaks
100 g (3¹⁄4 oz) clarified butter or oil (see Chef's tip)
800 ml (26 fl oz) brown stock (see page 63)
50 g (1³⁄4 oz) onion or French shallot, finely chopped
10 g (¹⁄4 oz) crushed black peppercorns
50 ml (1³⁄4 fl oz) white wine
50 ml (1³⁄4 fl oz) brandy
small sprigs of fresh parsley, to garnish

1 Season the steaks with salt. In a shallow frying pan big enough to fit the four steaks, heat the clarified butter or oil until hazing. Add the steaks and brown for about 3–4 minutes on each side for medium rare, and a little longer for medium. Remove from the pan, cover with aluminium foil to keep warm and set aside. For well- done steak, brown on each side for 3 minutes, then transfer to an ovenproof dish and bake in a moderately hot oven 200°C (400°F/Gas 6) for 8–10 minutes. Remove and cover with foil.

2 Add the stock to a medium pan and reduce down to about 400 ml (13 fl oz). Add the onion or shallot to the frying pan and lightly colour for 3–4 minutes before adding the peppercorns. Add the wine and half the brandy, stir with a wooden spoon to scrape the sticky meat juices from the base of the pan, mix them in and bubble for 1 minute until syrupy. Stir in the reduced stock and bring to the boil. Cook the sauce for 7 minutes, or until syrupy, then add the remaining brandy.

3 Return the steaks to the sauce in the pan and reheat for 3–4 minutes, without allowing the sauce to boil. Serve on individual warm plates or on one large plate. Garnish with parsley and serve with some chipped or roasted potatoes.

Chef's tip Clarified butter is used because it will cook at a higher temperature than normal butter without burning. You will need 180 g (5³⁄4 oz) butter to yield 100 g (3¹⁄4 oz) clarified butter. Melt the butter over low heat in a small, heavy-based pan, without stirring or shaking the pan. Skim the foam from the surface, then carefully pour the clear butter into a container, leaving the white sediment in the pan. Cover and refrigerate until needed. Will keep for up to 4 weeks.

Seafood stew

There is no substitute for fresh, good-quality ingredients, simply prepared as in this mouthwatering fish stew. These scallops, prawns and mushrooms cooked in white wine and cream are delicious served with crusty bread and a green salad.

Preparation time 20 minutes
Total cooking time 25 minutes
Serves 4

16 scallops, without shells
16 large raw prawns
1 large French shallot, chopped
250 ml (8 fl oz) white wine
sprig of fresh thyme
1 small bay leaf
240 g (7¹/₂ oz) button mushrooms, sliced
250 ml (8 fl oz) thick (double) cream
1 tablespoon chopped fresh parsley

1 Trim away the dark vein from the scallops and peel and devein the prawns, leaving the tails intact. Place the chopped shallot, white wine, thyme and bay leaf in a large pan with a tight-fitting lid. Bring to the boil and cook for 5 minutes. Add the scallops, prawns and mushrooms. Reduce the heat and simmer, covered, for 5–8 minutes, or until the scallops and prawns are cooked (they should be firm but not hard). Remove the scallops and prawns with a slotted spoon and keep warm.

2 Increase the heat to high and boil the cooking liquid for 5 minutes. Stir in the cream and cook for a further 5 minutes. Season to taste with salt and pepper. Return the seafood to the sauce and stir for 1 minute to heat through. Stir in the parsley and serve.

Veal chops grand-mère

Grand-mère, 'grandmother' in French, refers to the garnish of glazed onions, fried bacon, mushrooms and small potato balls that melt in the mouth, making this dish a nourishing and succulent meal.

Preparation time **30 minutes**
Total cooking time **1 hour 15 minutes**
Serves 4

80 ml (2³/4 fl oz) oil
30 g (1 oz) unsalted butter
4 veal chops, about 200 g (6¹/2 oz) each
250 g (8 oz) slab bacon, finely diced
300 g (10 oz) button mushrooms
300 g (10 oz) pearl or pickling onions
1 teaspoon sugar
800 g (1 lb 10 oz) potatoes
30 ml (1 fl oz) white wine
100 ml (3¹/4 fl oz) brown stock (see page 63)

1 Preheat the oven to warm 170°C (325°F/Gas 3). In a large flameproof casserole dish, heat 1 tablespoon of the oil, then add the butter. Cook the chops for 2–3 minutes each side, or until well browned. Remove from the dish and set aside. Add the bacon and cook until browned, remove from the dish and set aside. Add the mushrooms and cook, stirring occasionally, for about 2 minutes. Remove from the dish and set aside. Add the onions to a small pan with the sugar and cook, stirring occasionally, until lightly golden. Remove and set aside.

2 Peel the potatoes and scoop out small balls with a melon baller. Heat the remaining oil in a frying pan and cook the potatoes until golden brown, then drain on paper towels.

3 Pour the wine into the dish and stir well, scraping the bottom of the pan until the pan juices have dissolved. Cook until the wine has reduced by three quarters. Add the stock and 100 ml (3¹/4 fl oz) water, bring to the boil and cook until reduced by half.

4 Return the meat and vegetables to the casserole dish and toss to coat in the liquid. Season with salt and freshly ground black pepper. Cover and bake for about 30–40 minutes, or until the chops are tender and cooked through. Serve immediately.

Beef curry

Dark brown pieces of beef simmering in aromatic spices will fill you with anticipation long before the sauce has reached its required rich brown appearance. Serve with basmati rice, cucumber raita and mango chutney.

Preparation time **20 minutes**
Total cooking time **2 hours**

Serves 4

750 g (1 lb 8 oz) braising or stewing steak
2 tablespoons ghee or oil
1 large onion, thinly sliced
1 clove garlic, crushed
2 green chillies, seeded and sliced
1/4 teaspoon ground cloves
1 1/2 teaspoons ground coriander
1 teaspoon ground turmeric
1 teaspoon garam masala
1/2 teaspoon chilli powder
1 1/2 teaspoons ground cumin
1 teaspoon salt
375 ml (12 fl oz) brown stock (see page 63)
2 large tomatoes, peeled and finely chopped
150 ml (5 fl oz) coconut milk
200 g (6 1/2 oz) English spinach leaves
100 g (3 1/4 oz) natural yoghurt, stirred to smooth

1   Remove any fat or sinew from the beef and cut into 3 mm (1/8 inch) cubes. Heat the ghee or oil in a flameproof casserole dish over high heat. Add the beef and fry in batches for about 3 minutes, or until brown. Remove the beef and set aside. Add the onion and garlic to the casserole dish and cook for 2–3 minutes, or until soft. Reduce the heat, stir in the chillies, cloves, coriander, turmeric, garam masala, chilli powder, cumin and salt. Cook for about 2 minutes, stirring continuously. Add a few tablespoons of the stock at the end if it looks as if it may catch and burn.

2   Stir in the chopped tomato and return the beef to the dish. Add the stock to just below the level of the meat and bring to the boil. Cover and cook over low heat or in a warm 170°C (325°F/Gas 3) oven for 1 hour 20 minutes. Add a little more stock if the curry becomes too dry. Check that the meat is tender and cook for another 15–20 minutes if necessary. Add the coconut milk and spinach and cook for 10 minutes. Adjust the seasoning to taste.

3   Just before serving, stir the yoghurt into the curry to taste. Serve hot over basmati rice.

Chef's tip When browning the meat, make sure that there is only one layer of meat in the casserole dish and that the heat is high, otherwise the juices will run out of the meat and it will stew rather than brown.

Tarragon and tomato chicken casserole

This recipe comes from Lyon, France's third largest city and its gastronomic capital, situated close to the Burgundy vineyards.

Preparation time 20 minutes
Total cooking time 45 minutes
Serves 4

1 chicken, weighing 1.2 kg (2 lb 6¹/2 oz)
oil or butter, for cooking
200 ml (6¹/2 fl oz) tarragon vinegar (see Chef's tip)
1 kg (2 lb) tomatoes
15 g (¹/2 oz) unsalted butter, softened
15 g (¹/2 oz) plain flour
sprig of fresh tarragon, to garnish

1 Cut the chicken into four or eight pieces, following the method in the Chef's techniques on page 62, and season with salt and pepper. Heat a little oil or butter in a frying pan and brown the chicken on all sides, skin-side-down first. Do not overcrowd the pan so, if necessary, brown the chicken in batches. Remove the chicken and pour off any excess oil from the pan.

2 Return all the chicken to the pan and add half of the tarragon vinegar. Cover and simmer for 10 minutes.

Turn the chicken pieces over, cover and cook for a further 10 minutes, or until the juices run clear when pricked with a fork. Remove the chicken from the pan. Cover the pan and keep the sauce warm.

3 Score a cross in the base of each tomato, then plunge into boiling water for 10 seconds. Rinse with cold water and peel the skin away from the cross. Cut in half, remove the seeds, then cut into eighths. Put the remaining vinegar in a pan and boil for 4 minutes. Mix together the softened butter and flour, whisk into the reduced vinegar and then whisk this into the sauce. Return the chicken to the sauce, add the tomato and simmer for 10 minutes, or until the sauce just coats the back of a spoon. Check the seasoning. Chop the fresh tarragon just before serving, sprinkle over the casserole and serve with rice.

Chef's tip Make your own tarragon vinegar by placing a sprig of fresh tarragon in a bottle of ordinary red or white wine vinegar. After a week, strain out the tarragon and your vinegar is ready. All your favourite herbs can be used in this way.

Veal chops with Chablis en cocotte

A cocotte is a round or oval cooking pan with two handles and a tight-fitting cover that was traditionally used to cook slow-cooking dishes. Now 'en cocotte' refers to braised dishes in which the meat is first browned and then cooked in a liquid at a low simmer either in the oven or on the stove top.

*Preparation time **15 minutes***
*Total cooking time **50 minutes***
Serves 4

4 veal chops, about 200 g (6¹/₂ oz) each
60 g (2 oz) unsalted butter
300 g (10 oz) veal trimmings or bones, finely chopped
 (ask the butcher)
250 ml (8 fl oz) Chablis wine
bouquet garni (see page 63)
70 g (2¹/₄ oz) slab bacon, finely diced
I small onion, finely chopped
I carrot, finely diced
I turnip, finely diced
I tablespoon chopped fresh parsley

1 Season the veal chops with salt and pepper. In a large frying pan over medium heat, melt two thirds of the butter and brown the veal for 2–3 minutes on both sides. Once browned, transfer the chops to a plate. Add the trimmings to the pan and brown, then return the veal chops to the pan. Cover, reduce the heat and cook slowly for 4 minutes on each side. Transfer the chops and trimmings back to the plate and set aside. Increase the heat to medium-high and cook the meat juices, stirring constantly, for about 3–4 minutes, or until they have caramelised onto the bottom of the pan. Strain the trimmings to remove the excess fat and return to the pan. Add the Chablis and stir well, scraping the bottom, until the cooking juices have dissolved. Cook for about 5 minutes, or until the wine has reduced in volume by three quarters. Add 500 ml (16 fl oz) water and the bouquet garni and simmer for 30 minutes. Strain the sauce into a jug and discard the veal trimmings and bouquet garni.

2 Meanwhile, melt the remaining butter in another frying pan and brown the bacon for 2–3 minutes. Add the onion and carrot and cook for a further 2 minutes before adding the turnip. Reduce the heat, cover and cook for 8 minutes.

3 Add the sauce to the vegetables, bring to the boil and cook for 10 minutes. Transfer the veal chops into the hot sauce, reduce the heat and leave to simmer for about 5 minutes, or until the veal is heated through. Serve immediately, sprinkled with the chopped parsley.

Braised lamb with tomato sauce

A simple yet delicious lamb stew, flavoured with garlic, bacon and tomatoes, which can be served with rice or fresh pasta.

Preparation time **25 minutes**
Total cooking time **1 hour 45 minutes**
Serves 4

1.2 kg (2 lb 6¹/2 oz) lamb shoulder, boned, trimmed and cut into small pieces
2 tablespoons oil
40 g (1¹/4 oz) unsalted butter
60 g (2 oz) slab bacon, diced
I small onion, chopped
I small carrot, chopped
2 tablespoons tomato paste
I tablespoon plain flour
500 g (I lb) tomatoes, peeled, seeded and chopped
bouquet garni (see page 63)
4 cloves garlic, chopped
500 ml (16 fl oz) brown stock (see page 63) or water
I tablespoon chopped fresh parsley or basil

1 Preheat the oven to moderate 180°C (350°F/Gas 4). Season the lamb with salt and pepper. Heat the oil in a heavy-based frying pan over medium-high heat, add the lamb and brown it, in batches, for about 6–8 minutes, or until well coloured on all sides. Drain on paper towels.

2 Melt the butter in a large flameproof casserole dish over medium heat. Add the bacon and cook until golden brown. Add the onion and carrot and cook for about 3 minutes. Stir in the tomato paste and cook for a further 2 minutes. Sprinkle with the flour and bake for 5 minutes. Remove from the oven and mix in the flour. Add the tomatoes, bouquet garni and garlic. Place on the heat and cook for 5 minutes, stirring constantly, then add the stock or water. Bring to the boil, stirring constantly. Add the lamb, cover and bake for 1 hour, or until the meat is tender when pierced with the tip of a sharp knife.

3 Remove the meat from the sauce, cover and keep warm. Strain the sauce through a fine sieve, pressing well to extract as much liquid as possible. Discard the solids and pour the sauce into a pan.

4 Bring the sauce back to the boil, skimming if necessary. Simmer for 10 minutes, or until the sauce is thick enough to coat the back of a spoon. Add the lamb and stir until heated through. Season with salt and pepper. Sprinkle with the parsley or basil and serve.

Chef's techniques

◆

Jointing a chicken

The flavour of a dish will often be better if, rather than buying pieces, you cut up a whole bird. This method of jointing ensures even-sized portions, and you can cut the chicken into four or eight pieces.

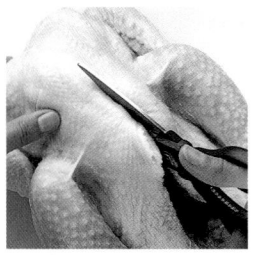

Use a pair of kitchen scissors to cut through the length of the breastbone.

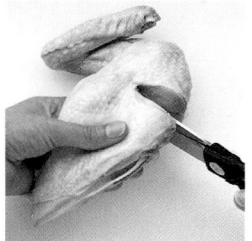

Cut through the top third of the breast, leaving two even-sized portions. You can also remove the wing tips at this stage, if you wish.

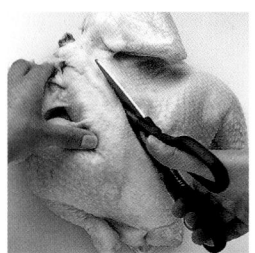

Turn the chicken over and cut down either side of the backbone to completely remove it. The backbone should come away in one piece.

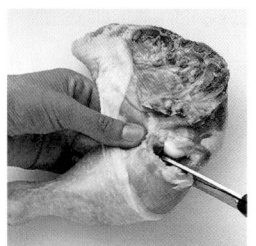

Separate the leg from the thigh by cutting through the leg joint.

Following the natural contours of the thigh, cut through to separate the breast and wing piece from the thigh and leg.

You now have eight equal-sized chicken portions.

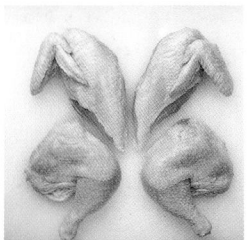

Repeat with the other half to produce four pieces.